Barefoot Muse
P R E S S

Selected Poems of Marceline Desbordes-Valmore

with an Essay by Paul Verlaine

Selected Poems

of Marceline Desbordes-Valmore

with an Essay by Paul Verlaine

Translated by
Anna M. Evans

Barefoot Muse Press
2014

First edition, 2014
Published by Barefoot Muse Press, www.barefootmuse.com

ISBN-13: 978-1492236122
ISBN-10: 1492236128

Printed in the United States of America

Acknowledgements

I wish to thank the Virginia Center for the Creative Arts, where this project was conceived and where many of the translations were begun. I would also like to thank Eugène Michel for his valuable assistance with Marceline's biography. Grateful acknowledgement is also made to the editors and publishers of the following publications in which these translated poems first appeared: "A Woman's Letter" in *Angle*, "Eastern Day," "Straight Talk and "What Did You Do With It?" in *Kin*, "To Delia (IV)" and "The Withered Wreath" in *Lucid Rhythms*, "When We're Apart" and "Anxiety" in *String Poet*, "My Room" in *Measure*.

Table of Contents

Introduction

Since 2009 I have been involved with the Mezzo Cammin Women Poets Timeline Project (www.mezzocammin.com/timeline), a sublimely ambitious project that ultimately aims to provide an online database of essays about every woman poet who ever published a book of poems. Many of the essays are generated as part of a critical seminar at the West Chester Poetry Conference, and somewhat on a whim I decided that for the 2013 seminar I would cover the lesser known French poet Marceline Desbordes-Valmore (1786-1859).

However, I had not really understood how little she was known, at least among anglophones. Whereas it feels like a new translation of Rimbaud's *Une saison en enfer* or Baudelaire's *Les fleurs du mal* comes out every five years or so, much of Desbordes-Valmore's vast oeuvre was simply unavailable in English translation, never mind in decent verse translation. The majority of biographical and critical prose was likewise only available in French, and thus what began for me as an exercise in research rapidly turned into an exercise in translation.

The essay included here by Paul Verlaine comes from his 1884 book, *Les Poètes Maudits*, in which it is worth noting that he accorded Desbordes-Valmore more space than anyone else, even his former lover Rimbaud. It is also interesting to observe how Verlaine's admiration for Desbordes-Valmore manages to come across despite his somewhat misogynistic and dismissive tone.

Some biographical information is no doubt in order. Marceline was born in 1786, the last of eight children (only four survived), in the Northern French town of Douai. Her father, Felix Desbordes, was a heraldic painter, who consequently lost his livelihood during the French revolution (1789-1799). Nevertheless Marceline considered her early childhood years idyllic, as illustrated by such poems as "Le berceau de Hélène" and "La fontaine."

The idyll ended abruptly when Marceline was ten, and her parents separated. Marceline went with her mother Catherine. Even at that young age Marceline was beautiful, with golden hair, an expressive face and a passable singing voice, so a year later Catherine determined to raise funds by putting her daughter on the stage, first at Lille, and later at Rochefort and Bordeaux.

In November 1801, Marceline and her mother embarked on a ship to Guadeloupe, supposedly to seek financial aid from a cousin of Catherine's who had married a wealthy plantation owner. In May 1802 the women finally arrived in Guadeloupe, only to find the cousin a widow, and the plantation in mutinous ruins. Catherine died of yellow fever exacerbated by disappointment and remorse, obliging the sixteen-year-old Marceline to return to France alone, a feat that she somewhat incredibly managed to accomplish.

Marceline rejoined the Lille troupe and went back on the stage, supporting her family by sending them money when she could. Because of her stage career, Marceline became romantically involved with several men and gave birth to two children outside of marriage: in 1806 a daughter, believed to be the child of Louis Lacour, who died at three weeks; and in 1810, a son, Marie-Eugène, more reliably assumed to be the son of Eugène Debonne, with whom Marceline lived for four years, who died at the age of five. Other men whose names are linked with Marceline's include Hilarion Audibert and Henri de Latouche.

Marceline's uneven romantic life and the losses of her babies would seem to be the impetus that caused Marceline to begin writing poetry, and indeed her first collection, *Elégies et Romances*, which was published in 1819, contains many poems which seem to relate the story of an unhappy love affair, including "L'inquiétude", "L'adieu du soir" and "La sincere," although subsequent editions from 1820 onward re-ordered the poems, obscuring any narrative thread. The collection was well received and ultimately opened doors for her in the literary world so that she was able to give up the theater and write full-time. Further collections of poetry followed, along with novels and poems for children.

In 1817, Marceline married a younger actor, Francois-Prosper Lanchantin, whose stage name was Valmore. Another daughter, who died at three weeks, was born ten months later, their son Hippolyte in 1820, and their daughter Ondine, who died in her early thirties, in 1821. Their last child, Ines, was born in 1825 and died aged twenty-one. This litany of loss is apparent in later poems such as "Les sanglots" and "La couronne effeuillé." The couple were never wealthy and Valmore continued to act in traveling companies, even dragging the family to Italy for a season, until well into his fifties. At last the Valmores retired to Paris, living modestly until Marceline died of cancer in 1859.

In putting together this short selection, I have attempted to represent Marceline's work broadly (excluding her children's poetry) while at the same time providing examples of poems where her talents are most original and effective. Out of scholarly diligence I also translated the poems Verlaine quotes at length, most of which were not published in her lifetime.

Verlaine praises Marceline for using "to great effect uncommon rhythms such as eleven syllable lines, among others"—a practice he was later to adopt and promote, and indeed for which he was credited. To understand the significance of this it is necessary to examine briefly the prevalence and influence of the twelve-syllable Alexandrine line. The Alexandrine was traditionally end-stopped and demonstrated a strong central caesura—in other words the sixth syllable never arose in the middle of a word, and preferably preceded punctuation, as in this example from Racine:

> Ou suis-je? | qu'ai-je fait? || que dois-je | faire encore?
> Quel transport | me saisit? || quel chagrin | me devore?

Note how either side of the caesura, the phrases seem to split again into two groupings, each of three syllables.

As William Rees states, in his introduction to the Penguin Book of French Poetry 1820-1950: "The haunting, lyrical Impair line of 5, 7, 9 or 11 units, [is] extolled and demonstrated beautifully by Verlaine above all." But Verlaine learned from Marceline how this eleven-syllable line arises, for example, when a two-syllable grouping is substituted for a three-syllable, as in the first grouping of the line given below:

> Ne peuvent | me sauver | de la long|ueur du temps.

Nor does a simple syllable count really describe Marceline's "uncommon rhythms" sufficiently. What she appears to be doing in poems like "L'inquiétude" is generating three syllable groupings where typically the first two syllables are shorter and the third more drawn out—I hesitate to use the word anapest to describe the meter of a language where stress is known not to be the significant determinant. I have, however, taken the liberty of translating such poems into anapestic tetrameter.

Much has been made of the fact that Marceline Desbordes-Valmore was largely unschooled and self-taught. She also came to poetry by way of music—first as a singer and later as a guitar player—and this subconscious musicality, combined with her freedom from academically proscribed strictures, permitted her to break the alexandrine with impunity. I have translated these poems into anapestic tetrameter.

Marceline also experimented to great effect with shorter lines and unusual cross-stanza/identity rhyme schemes, as seen in poems like "La sincere," "Qu'en avez vous fait?" and "À Délie (IV)." Even allowing for the overuse of sentimental tropes common to the era—"coeur" appears 24 times in the poems I translated—such shorter lines give these poems a gritty, contemporary feel.

It is therefore unsurprising that despite a historical lack of attention from English-speaking critics, Marceline Desbordes-Valmore's work has never ceased to be popular in her homeland. I hope that this small book may go some way toward bringing her the attention she deserves from the rest of the world.

~ Anna M. Evans, Hainesport, August 2013

Marceline Desbordes-Valmore
by Paul Verlaine

(from "Les Poetes Maudits")

Marceline Desbordes-Valmore

In spite of the effect of a few articles, one very detailed by the marvelous Sainte-Beuve[i], the other perhaps, dare we say it? a little too short by Baudelaire, even in spite of a kind of good public opinion which does not compare her totally with the distant Louise Collet, Amable Tastu, Anais Segalas and other unimportant blue stockings, (we are forgetting Loisa Puget, in addition, it would seem she can be amusing, for those who like that sort of thing), Marceline Desbordes-Valmore has deserved, through her seeming yet absolute obscurity, to be placed among our *Accursed Poets*, and from henceforth it seems to us to be essential to speak of her in as much length and detail as possible.

In the past, M. Barbey d'Aurevilly[ii] has brought her out of the ranks and pointed out, with that strange skill he possesses, her own strangeness, and the genuine, if feminine, ability that she had.

As for us, notwithstanding our interest in good or beautiful poetry, we were ignorant of her, contenting ourselves with the word of the masters, when Arthur Rimbaud, to be precise, got to know us and practically forced us to read *everything* that we believed to be a jumble with some beauty within.

Our vast astonishment needs some time to explain.

First of all Marceline Desbordes-Valmore was actually from the North and not from the South of France, a distinction one was not aware of. What is believed to be from the North is usually thought well of (The sunny South of France is even better, but this kind of better can above all be the enemy of the genuine,)—and this pleases us because we are believed to be from the North too, in the end!

Next, she is no pedant and has a good enough use of language, along with expending enough effort so that she does not show herself up as a mere businesswoman. Quotations will provide evidence of this self-asserted wisdom.

While we are waiting for them, can we revisit this total absence of the South of France in this relatively large body of work? And besides that, understand as passionately as possible her Spanish North, (but doesn't Spain have a composure, an arrogance, even colder than Britain's?) Her North

Où vinrent s'asseoir les ferventes Espagnes.[iii]

Yes, none of that grandiloquence, none of that fakeness, none of that bad faith which one must disparage among the most obvious work from across the Loire. And nevertheless it's all so warm—these romances of her youth, these memories of womanhood, these maternal fears! And gentle, and sincere, and everything! What landscapes, what love of landscapes!! And though this love is chaste and discreet, it is nevertheless fierce and moving!

We have said that Marceline Desbordes-Valmore's language was good enough, it has to be said that it is very much good enough; only we ourselves are such purists, such pedants, that we must add, before someone calls us decadent, (an insult to take on the chin, between parentheses, during a picturesque sunset in fall) that a certain naïveté without any stylistic ingenuity could occasionally awaken our literary prejudices which aim at perfection. The truth of our reassessment will be brought to light in the course of the quotations we are going to produce.

Still the chaste yet fierce passion that we have pointed out, the almost excessive emotion that we have praised, mean it needs to be said, without overstatement, no! after a somber reading of our first paragraphs from the necessity of being conscientious, that we support their opinion of her.

And here is the proof:

Une Lettre de Femme[iv]

Les femmes, je le sais, ne doivent pas écrire ;
J'écris pourtant,
Afin que dans mon coeur au loin tu puisses lire
Comme en partant.

Je ne tracerai rien qui ne soit dans toi-même
Beaucoup plus beau :
Mais le mot cent fois dit, venant de ce qu'on aime,
Semble nouveau.

Qu'il te porte au bonheur ! Moi, je reste à l'attendre,
Bien que, là-bas,
Je sens que je m'en vais, pour voir et pour entendre
Errer tes pas.

Ne te détourne point s'il passe une hirondelle
Par le chemin,
Car je crois que c'est moi qui passerai, fidèle,
Toucher ta main.

Tu t'en vas, tout s'en va ! Tout se met en voyage,
Lumière et fleurs,
Le bel été te suit, me laissant à l'orage,
Lourde de pleurs.

Mais si l'on ne vit plus que d'espoir et d'alarmes,
Cessant de voir,
Partageons pour le mieux : moi, je retiens les larmes,
Garde l'espoir.

Non, je ne voudrais pas, tant je te suis unie,
Te voir souffrir :
Souhaiter la douleur à sa moitié bénie,
C'est se haïr.

Isn't this divine? But wait!

Jour d'Orient [v]

Ce fut un jour pareil à ce beau jour
Que, pour tout perdre, incendiait l'amour !

C'était un jour de charité divine
Où dans l'air bleu l'éternité chemine ;
Où dérobée à son poids étouffant
La terre joue et redevient enfant ;
C'était partout comme un baiser de mère,
Long rêve errant dans une heure éphémère ;
Heure d'oiseaux, de parfums, de soleil,
D'oubli de tout... hors du bien sans pareil.
.   .   .   .   .   .

Ce fut un jour pareil à ce beau jour
Que, pour tout perdre, incendiait l'amour !

We must restrain ourselves, and keep our quotations for a different purpose.

And, before moving onto to the strictest test of sublimity, if it is allowed to speak thus of a part of the work of this adorable sweet woman, let us, literally with tears in our eyes, recite this from her pen:

Renoncement [vi]

Pardonnez-moi, Seigneur, mon visage attristé,
Vous qui l'aviez formé de sourire et de charmes ;
Mais sous le front joyeux vous aviez mis les larmes,

Et de vos dons, Seigneur, ce don seul m'est resté.

C'est le mois envié, c'est le meilleur peut-être :
Je n'ai plus à mourir à mes liens de fleurs ;
Ils vous sont tous rendus, cher auteur de mon être,
Et je n'ai plus à moi que le sel de mes pleurs.

Les fleurs sont pour l'enfant ; le sel est pour la femme ;
Faites-en l'innocence et trempez-y mes jours.
Seigneur ! quand tout ce sel aura lavé mon âme,
Vous me rendrez un coeur pour vous aimer toujours !

Tous mes étonnements sont finis sur la terre,
Tous mes adieux sont faits, l'âme est prête à jaillir,
Pour atteindre à ses fruits protégés de mystère
Que la pudique mort a seule osé cueillir,

O Sauveur ! soyez tendre au moins à d'autres mères,
Par amour pour la vôtre et par pitié pour nous !
Baptisez leurs enfants de nos larmes amères,
Et relevez les miens tombés à vos genoux !

How this sadness transcends that of Olympio[vii] and "To Olympio,"[viii] however beautiful (especially the last) these two overly proud poems may be! But, dear readers, forgive us, on the threshold of other sanctuaries within this church of a hundred chapels, for chanting with you after us:

Que mon nom ne soit rien qu'une ombre douce et vaine,
Qu'il ne cause jamais ni l'effroi ni la peine !
Qu'un indigent l'emporte après m'avoir parlé
Et le garde longtemps dans son coeur consolé !

Have you forgiven us?

And now, let us turn to the mother, the daughter, the young daughter, and the troubled but deeply devout Christian that was the poet Marceline Desbordes-Valmore.

***

We have said that we shall try to speak of the poet in all her aspects.

Let us proceed in order, and, we are sure you will be pleased with this, using as many examples as possible. Therefore here to begin with are some abusively long specimens by the young romantic girl from 1820, like a better Parny[ix], in a form scarcely different, yet nevertheless developing in an entirely different manner.

L'Inquiétude[x]

Qu'est-ce donc qui me trouble, et qu'est-ce que j'attends ?
Je suis triste à la ville, et m'ennuie au village ;
Les plaisirs de mon âge
Ne peuvent me sauver de la longueur du temps.

Autrefois l'amitié, les charmes de l'étude
Remplissaient sans effort mes paisibles loisirs.
Oh ! quel est donc l'objet de mes vagues désirs ?
Je l'ignore, et le cherche avec inquiétude.
Si pour moi le bonheur n'était pas la gaîté,
Je ne le trouve plus dans ma mélancolie ;
Mais, si je crains les pleurs autant que la folie,
Où trouver la félicité ?

.   .   .   .

Next she addresses her "Reason", commanding and renouncing it at the same time, very gently! Above the rest, we admire for our part this monologue in the manner of Corneille[xi] which seems more tender than Racine but dignified and proud in the style of both great poets though with a whole other angle.

Among a thousand sweetnesses occasionally soppy, but never dull and always astonishing, we beg you during this rapid examination to look at several isolated lines with the aim of tempting you to read the entire thing.

.   .   .   .
Cache-moi ton regard plein d'âme et de tristesse[xii]

.   .   .   .
On ressemble au plaisir sous un chapeau de fleurs[xiii]

.   .   .   .
Inexplicable cœur, énigme pour toi-même[xiv]

.   .   .   .
Dans ma sécurité tu ne vois qu'un delire[xv]

.   .   .   .
         . Trop faible esclave, écoute,

Ecoute et ma raison te pardonne et t'absout.
Rends-lui du moins les pleurs! Tu vas céder sans doute?
Hélas non! toujours non! O mon cœur, prends donc tout![xvi]

As for "The Lost Prayer," the poem from which these last few lines are taken, we are making honorable amends for just a moment on account of the word "sweet" which we have over-used. With Marceline Desbordes-Valmore one hardly knows what one should say or not say, this genius troubles you so deliciously, enchanting even the sorcerer himself!

If anything about passion has been as well-expressed as by the best elegies, it's indeed this, or we don't want to know anything more about it.

And of the pure friendships and at the same time chaste loves of this tender and haughty woman, how can one describe them well enough except to offer the advice to read her complete work? Listen once again to these two short excerpts:

Les Deux Amours[xvii]

C'était l'amour plus folâtre que tender;
D'un trait sans force il effleura mon cœur;
Il fut léger comme un riant mensonge.

.   .   .   .
Il offrit le plaisir sans parler de Bonheur.[xviii]

.   .   .   .
C'est dans tes yeux que je vis l'autre amour[xix]

.   .   .   .   .   .
Cet entier oubli de soi-même,
Ce besoin d'aimer pour aimer
Et que le mot aimer semble a peine exprimer
Ton cœur seul le renferme et le mien le devine.
Je sens à tes transports, à ma fidélité,
Qu'il veut dire a la fois Bonheur, éternité,
Et que sa puissance est divine.[xx]

Les deux amitiés[xxi]

Il est deux Amitiés comme il est deux Amours.
L'une ressemble à l'imprudence ;
C'est une enfant qui rit toujours.

And in charming manner it describes divinely the friendship of two little girls. Then,

L'autre Amitié, plus grave, plus austère,
Se donne avec lenteur, choisit avec mystère ;[xxii]

. . . .
Elle écarte les fleurs, de peur de s'y blesser.[xxiii]

. . . .
Elle voit par ses yeux et marche sur ses pas :
Elle attend, et ne prévient pas.[xxiv]

Here is the serious note.

***

Alas, how discontented we will be, once we have finished this study. What pleasant and local marvels! What scenery of Arras and Douai![xxv] What banks of the Scarpe! How sweet and somewhat odd (we hear ourselves and you understand us) these young Albertines, these Ines, these Ondines, this Laly Galine,[xxvi] these exquisite "my beautiful country, my fresh birthplace, pure air of my green homeland, be well, sweet center of the universe."

However we must keep our poor examination of a truly great poet within the fair (or unfair) limits that cold logic imposes on the desired size of our little book. But—but! What a shame to confine ourselves to only quoting fragments like these, written well before Lamartine[xxvii] burst forth and which are, we insist on it, like a chaste and peaceful Parny!

Dieu! qu'il est tard! quelle surprise!
Le temps a fui comme un éclair;
Douze fois l'heure a frappé l'air.
Et près de toi je suis encore assise ;
Et, loin de pressentir le moment du sommeil.
Je croyais voir encore un rayon de soleil !

Se peut-il que déjà l'oiseau dorme au bocage?
Ah ! pour dormir il fait si beau !

. . . .
Garde-toi d'éveiller notre chien endormi ;
Il méconnaîtrait son ami,
Et de mon imprudence il instruirait ma mère.

. . . .
Écoute la raison, va-t'en. Laisse ma main !
Il est minuit...[xxviii]

Is it pure, this "let go of my hand," is it romantic, this "it is midnight," after this ray of light that she thinks she still sees!

Let us, even as we sigh, leave the young girl. We saw the woman at the start of this, what a woman! Such a friend! The poem on the death of Madame de Girardin![xxix]

La mort vient de fermer les plus beaux yeux du monde.[xxx]

The mother!

Quand j'ai gronde mon fils je me cache et je pleure.[xxxi]

And when this son goes to college, it requires an agonized scream, doesn't it?

Candeur de mon enfant, comme on va vous detruire[xxxii]

The least ignored works by Marceline Desbordes-Valmore are her adorable fables, unluckily for her, which are after the manner of bitter old La Fontaine[xxxiii] and the nicer Florian[xxxiv]:

Un tout petit enfant s'en allait a l'école;
On avait dit: allez! Il tachait d'obéir.[xxxv]

And "The Little Fraidy Cat" and "The Little Liar!"
Oh we beg you, stop with these dull and affected niceties!

Si mon enfant m'aime,[xxxvi]

sings "The Sleeper," which we want to call here "The Lullaby," since this would be a much better title.

Dieu dira lui-même:
J'aime cet enfant qui dort.
Qu'on lui porte un rêve d'or.[xxxvii]

But, noting that Marceline Desbordes-Valmore—the first poet of her age to do so—used to great effect uncommon rhythms such as eleven syllable lines, among others, and that she was a great artist without being too self-conscious and so much the better for that, let us resume our admiration with this fantastic poem.

[Verlaine here quotes the entire French text of "Les Sanglots" ("The Tears"), which can be found in full and with translation starting on page 55.]

Here we let our pen fall and delightful tears dampen our spidery scrawl. We find ourselves powerless to dissect such an angel any longer!

And, pedantically, because it is our pitiful role, we announce in a loud and clear voice that Marceline Desbordes-Valmore is, quite simply—along with George Sand[xxxviii], so different, long-lasting, though not without charming self-indulgencies, of serious common sense, of pride, and one might as well add attractive to men—the only woman of genius and talent from this century and from all the centuries in the company perhaps of Sappho, and of Saint Therese.

---

[i] Charles Augustin Sainte-Beuve (1804-1869) who wrote the introduction to the 1860 posthumous *Poésies*

[ii] Jules Amédée Barbey d'Aurevilly (1808-1889), French novelist, short story writer and critic

[iii] "Where fervent Spaniards came to settle themselves." This line is from "Rêve intermittent d'une nuit triste" ("Intermittent Dream During a Sad Night").

[iv] See translation on pg 25

[v] See translation on page 17

[vi] See translation on page 53

[vii] "Tristesse d'Olympio" by Victor Hugo

[viii] "To Olympio" by Victor Hugo

[ix] Evariste de Parny (1753-1814)

[x] Translation on page 23

[xi] Pierre Corneille (1606-1684)

[xii] "Hide from me your soulful saddened look" from "Le Regard" ("The Look").

[xiii] "We look like we're happy beneath a flowered hat" from "Le Chien D'Olivier" ("Oliver's Dog").

[xiv] The next few quotations are all from "La prière perdue" (The Lost Prayer"). "Unexplainable heart, an enigma even to yourself"

[xv] " When I am safe you're just looking for thrills"

[xvi] "Listen, too weak slave, Listen! And my reason will forgive and absolve you: At least give it tears! There's no doubt you'll give in? Alas no! Always no! O my heart, take it all!"

[xvii] "The Two Loves." It was a love more playful than tender; With a soft stroke it brushed my heart; It was light as a false laugh."

[xviii] "It offered pleasure without speaking of luck."

[xix] "It was in your eyes that I saw the other love."

[xx] "This complete loss of self, this need to love for love's sake, and that the word love scarcely seems adequate, your heart alone confirms and my heart guesses. I feel from your delights and from my faithfulness that it needs to say at the same time good luck, eternity and that its power is divine."

---

xxi Verlaine has omitted line 3 without signaling the omission: "Faite pour l'âge heureux dont elle a l'ignorance." The entire excerpt can be translated: "Two Friendships. There are two friendships like there are two loves. One looks like imprudence; made for the age of innocence, it's a child that's always laughing."

xxii "The other friendship, more serious and severe, gives itself slowly, chooses mysteriously."

xxiii "It moves flowers aside out of fear of hurting them."

xxiv Verlaine has omitted the penultimate line of the poem without signaling the omission: " Son abord est craintif, son regard est timide ;" The final 3 lines of the poem can be translated "It sees with [reason's] eyes and walks in his footsteps; its aspect is fearful, its look timid. It waits, and does not anticipate."

xxv Marceline was born in Douai, which is located on the River Scarpe about 25 km from the town of Arras, close to France's Northern border

xxvi Names of Marceline's childhood friends and sister

xxvii Alphonse de Lamartine (1790-1869), French writer, poet and politician.

xxviii This excerpt comes from "L'Adieu du soir" ("Farewell to Evening.") See translation on page 19

xxix Delphine de Girardin (1804-1855), French author. The poem is "Madame Emile de Girardin"

xxx "Death has just closed the most beautiful eyes in the world."

xxxi " When I've rebuked my son, I hide and cry." From "Hippolyte," full translation on page 47

xxxii "Innocence of my child, how you will be destroyed." The poem is "A mon fils," ("To My Son.")

xxxiii Jean de La Fontaine (1621-1695), French poet and fabulist

xxxiv Jean-Pierre Claris de Florian (1755-1794), French Poet and romance writer

xxxv "A very small child set off toward school; They had told him to go, and he tried to obey." From "L'ecolier", ("The Schoolboy.")

xxxvi "If my child loves me."

xxxvii "God will say to himself: I love this sleeping child. Let him be sent a golden dream."

xxxviii George Sand, pseudonym of Amantine Lucile Aurore Dupin (1804-1876), French novelist and memoirist.

Selected Poems
of Marceline Desbordes-Valmore

(Translated by Anna M. Evans)

Jour d'Orient

Ce fut un jour pareil à ce beau jour
Que, pour tout perdre, incendiait l'amour!

C'était un jour de charité divine
Où dans l'air bleu l'éternité chemine;
Où dérobée à son poids étouffant
La terre joue et redevient enfant;
C'était partout comme un baiser de mère,
Long rêve errant dans une heure éphémère;
Heure d'oiseaux, de parfums, de soleil,
D'oubli de tout... hors du bien sans pareil.

Nous étions deux!... C'est trop d'un quand on aime
Pour se garder... Hélas! nous étions deux.
Pas un témoin qui sauve de soi-même!
Jamais au monde on n'eut plus besoin d'eux
Que nous l'avions! Lui, trop près de mon âme,
Avec son âme éblouissait mes yeux;
J'étais aveugle à cette double flamme,
Et j'y vis trop quand je revis les cieux.

Pour me sauver, j'étais trop peu savante;
Pour l'oublier... je suis encor vivante!

C'était un jour pareil à ce beau jour
Que, pour tout perdre, incendiait l'amour!

Eastern Day

It was a day like this one, just as bright,
which set this love, with all to lose, alight.

It was a day of perfect charity,
in whose blue breezes strolls eternity,
where, freed from the stifling loads it has to bear,
the earth can play, a child without a care.
It was like a mother's kiss in every place,
a long dream straying as time draws on apace,
an hour of birds, of perfumes, and of sun,
of utter forgetting, well-being bettered by none.

There were two of us. It's too much for one in love
to preserve oneself. Alas, that we were two!
Not one lone witness who had to think of himself.
We needed one so much—more than I knew
in all the world. Too close to my soul he came,
his soul's perfection dazzling my eyes.
I was struck blind by his own pair, aflame,
and saw too much when I looked back at the skies.

I was too dumb to recognize the threat.
I stay alive in order to forget.

It was a day like this one, just as bright,
which set this love, with all to lose, alight.

L'adieu du soir

Dieu! qu'il est tard! quelle surprise!
Le temps a fui comme un éclair;
Douze fois l'heure a frappé l'air.
Et près de toi je suis encore assise;
Et, loin de pressentir le moment du sommeil.
Je croyais voir encore un rayon de soleil!

Se peut-il que déjà l'oiseau dorme au bocage?
Ah! pour dormir il fait si beau!
Les étoiles en feu brillent dans le ruisseau,
Et le ciel n'a pas un nuage.
On dirait que c'est pour l'Amour
Qu'une si belle nuit a remplacé le jour!
Mais, il le faut, regagne ta chaumière;
Garde-toi d'éveiller notre chien endormi;
Il méconnaîtrait son ami,
Et de mon imprudence il instruirait ma mère.
Tu ne me réponds pas; tu détournes les yeux!
Hélas! tu veux en vain me cacher ta tristesse!
Tout ce qui manque à ta tendresse
Ne manque-t-il pas à mes vœux?
De te quitter donne-moi le courage;
Écoute la raison, va-t'en. Laisse ma main!
Il est minuit; tout repose au village.
Et nous voilà presqu'à demain!
Écoute! si le soir nous cause un mal extrême,
Bientôt le jour saura nous réunir,
Et le bonheur du souvenir
Va se confondre encore avec le bonheur même.

Mais, je le sens, j'ai beau compter sur ton retour.
En te disant adieu chaque soir je soupire;
Ah! puissions-nous bientôt désapprendre à le dire!
Ce mot, ce triste mot n'est pas fait pour l'amour!

Evening Farewell

My God! It's late! I'm so surprised!
Time has flown by lightning-quick.
Twelve times now the hour has struck
and I'm still sitting by your side.
But far from sensing day is almost done
I seem to see one last small ray of sun.

Can the bird be already asleep in the woods?
Ah! It's a fine night for a dream!
The fiery stars shine on top of the stream
and the sky is empty of clouds.
One could say that it is Love's way
for such a fine night to replace the day.
But you must go back to your bed;
beware of waking our sleeping dog up;
he doesn't like me much,
and he'll tell my mother I'm easily led.
You don't reply. Your eyes look somewhere new.
Alas! You wish in vain to hide your sadness.
Everything missed by your tenderness
don't you know I miss it too?
Give me the courage to say this farewell;
listen to reason. Go! Put my hand down.
It's midnight. In the village everything's still
and tomorrow is practically now!
Listen! If the evening causes such pain,
we'll be together soon in the light
and the remembered happiness of tonight
will merge with our real happiness again.

But I fear I count too much upon your return.
Each night with my goodbye to you I grieve.
If only saying it was something to unlearn!
This word, this sad word was not made for love.

Les séparés

N'écris pas—Je suis triste, et je voudrais m'éteindre
Les beaux étés sans toi, c'est la nuit sans flambeau
J'ai refermé mes bras qui ne peuvent t'atteindre,
Et frapper à mon cœur, c'est frapper au tombeau.
       N'écris pas!

N'écris pas—N'apprenons qu'à mourir à nous-mêmes
Ne demande qu'à Dieu ... qu'à toi, si je t'aimais!
Au fond de ton silence écouter que tu m'aimes,
C'est entendre le ciel sans y monter jamais.
       N'écris pas!

N'écris pas—Je te crains; j'ai peur de ma mémoire;
Elle a gardé ta voix qui m'appelle souvent
Ne montre pas l'eau vive à qui ne peut la boire
Une chère écriture est un portrait vivant.
       N'écris pas!

N'écris pas ces mots doux que je n'ose plus lire:
Il semble que ta voix les répand sur mon cœur;
Et que je les vois brûler à travers ton sourire;
Il semble qu'un baiser les empreint sur mon cœur.
       N'écris pas!

When We're Apart

Don't write—I'm upset and I wish I could die.
The summers without you are nights full of gloom.
I have folded my arms that can't touch you close by
and to knock on my heart is to knock on a tomb.
      Don't write!

Don't write—let us learn how to die while apart.
Ask God...or yourself...only this: did I love?
From the depths of your silence to hear your true heart
is to hear, without reaching, the heavens above.
      Don't write!

Don't write, for I fear you, my memory's cursed me;
it's imprisoned your voice, which still calls out my name.
Don't hold out fresh water to one who is thirsty.
A piece of fond writing can surely inflame.
      Don't write!

Don't write the words I've not dared read for a while.
It feels like your voice spreads them over my heart
and I watch them burn off as they bypass your smile,
and it seems like a kiss brands them onto my heart.
      Don't write!

L'inquiétude.

Qu'est-ce donc qui me trouble, et qu'est-ce que j'attends?
Je suis triste à la ville, et m'ennuie au village;
      Les plaisirs de mon âge
Ne peuvent me sauver de la longueur du temps.

Autrefois l'amitié, les charmes de l'étude
Remplissaient sans effort mes paisibles loisirs.
Oh! quel est donc l'objet de mes vagues désirs?
Je l'ignore, et le cherche avec inquiétude.
Si pour moi le bonheur n'était pas la gaîté,
Je ne le trouve plus dans ma mélancolie;
Mais, si je crains les pleurs autant que la folie,
      Où trouver la félicité?

Et vous qui me rendiez heureuse,
Avez-vous résolu de me fuir sans retour?
Répondez, ma raison; incertaine et trompeuse,
M'abandonnerez-vous au pouvoir de l'Amour? ...
Hélas! voilà le nom que je tremblais d'entendre.
Mais l'effroi qu'il inspire est un effroi si doux!
Raison, vous n'avez plus de secret à m'apprendre,
Et ce nom, je le sens, m'en a dit plus que vous.

Anxiety

What's this that upsets me? For what do I wait?
in the town, too much grief; out of it, too much leisure.
      What passes for modern pleasure
Can't save me from how every hour seems to grate.

Once there was friendship, the charms of a book
filled without effort each peaceful spare hour.
Oh what is the object of this vague desire?
I ignore it, but worry then makes me go look.
If my happiness wasn't with gaiety bound,
then nor am I finding it resting with sadness,
but if I fear weeping the same way as madness,
      then where is enjoyment found?

And you who might give me the thing that I'm needing,
have you truly decided to leave me forever?
Speak to me, Reason, uncertain, misleading,
will you now let the power of love take me over?
Alas, there's the name that I tremble to hear!
But the fear it inspires feels so gentle and true.
Reason, you have no more secrets to share,
and I think this name's told me more of them than you!

Une lettre de femme

Les femmes, je le sais, ne doivent pas écrire;
    J'écris pourtant,
Afin que dans mon cœur au loin tu puisses lire
    Comme en partant.

Je ne tracerai rien qui ne soit dans toi-même
    Beaucoup plus beau:
Mais le mot cent fois dit, venant de ce qu'on aime,
    Semble nouveau.

Qu'il te porte au bonheur! Moi, je reste à l'attendre,
    Bien que, là-bas,
Je sens que je m'en vais, pour voir et pour entendre
    Errer tes pas.

Ne te détourne point s'il passe une hirondelle
    Par le chemin,
Car je crois que c'est moi qui passerai, fidèle,
    Toucher ta main.

Tu t'en vas, tout s'en va ! Tout se met en voyage,
    Lumière et fleurs,
Le bel été te suit, me laissant à l'orage,
    Lourde de pleurs.

Mais si l'on ne vit plus que d'espoir et d'alarmes,
    Cessant de voir,
Partageons pour le mieux: moi, je retiens les larmes,
    Garde l'espoir.

Non, je ne voudrais pas, tant je te suis unie,
    Te voir souffrir:
Souhaiter la douleur à sa moitié bénie,
    C'est se haïr.

A Woman's Letter

I know that women aren't required to write;
        Yet write I do.
So my heart's words can reach your far-off sight
        as I want them to.

I'll pen nothing that wouldn't sound much better
        coming from you.
But from someone you love even a clichéd letter
        can seem new.

May it bring luck! Myself I'll stay aware
        until, over yonder
I feel that I must go to see and hear
        your footsteps wander.

Don't turn back if a swallow passes you
        as you cross the land—
I think it's faithful me flying by you to
        touch your hand.

When you go, it all goes. Everything sails,
        light and flowers.
Summer follows you, leaves me the gales
        heavy with tears.

Yet, if we see nothing but hope and fears,
        ceasing to see
is what I'd give to you. I'll keep my tears
        and hope, for me.

No, I don't want to see you the least depressed,
        my better half.
Close as I am to you, to wish you distressed
        is to hate myself.

La sincère.

Ah! c'est vous que je vois
Enfin! et cette voix qui parle est votre voix!
Pourquoi le sort mit-il mes jours si loin des vôtres?
J'ai tant besoin de vous pour oublier les autres! ~ *Victor Hugo* .

Veux-tu l'acheter?
Mon cœur est à vendre.
Veux-tu l'acheter,
Sans nous disputer?

Dieu l'a fait d'aimant;
Tu le feras tendre;
Dieu l'a fait d'aimant
Pour un seul amant!

Moi, j'en fais le prix;
Veux-tu le connaître?
Moi, j'en fais le prix;
N'en sois pas surpris:

As-tu tout le tien?
Donne! et sois mon maître.
As-tu tout le tien,
Pour payer le mien?

S'il n'est plus à toi,
Je n'ai qu'une envie;
S'il n'est plus à toi,
Tout est dit pour moi.

Le mien glissera,
Fermé dans la vie;
Le mien glissera,
Et Dieu seul l'aura!

Car, pour nos amours,
La vie est rapide;
Car, pour nos amours,
Elle a peu de jours.

Straight Talk

"Ah! I see you at last
and the voice that speaks is your dear voice, of course!
Why does fate set my days this far from yours?
My need for you is great so I'll forget the rest!"~ Victor Hugo

Would you like to buy it?
My heart is for sale.
Would you like to buy it,
no haggling over it?

God's made it a lover's,
you'll make it your own;
God's made it a lover's
for one lover alone.

I've set the price;
would you like to know it?
I've set the price;
don't be surprised.

Do you still have yours?
Be mine and show it.
Do you still have yours?
For mine costs yours.

If yours is gone,
I want one thing only;
If yours is gone
my life is done.

My own will slip from me,
shut in and lonely;
my own will slip from me,
God will have it from me.

Since, for love affairs,
life won't slow its pace;
since for love affairs
it allows few days.

L'âme doit courir
Comme une eau limpide;
L'âme doit courir,
Aimer et mourir.

The soul has to fly
as a stream must race;
the soul has to fly,
fall in love and die.

Qu'en avez-vous fait ?

Vous aviez mon cœur,
Moi, j'avais le vôtre:
Un cœur pour un cœur;
Bonheur pour bonheur!

Le vôtre est rendu,
Je n'en ai plus d'autre,
Le vôtre est rendu,
Le mien est perdu!

La feuille et la fleur
Et le fruit lui-même,
La feuille et la fleur,
L'encens, la couleur:

Qu'en avez-vous fait,
Mon maître suprême?
Qu'en avez-vous fait,
De ce doux bienfait?

Comme un pauvre enfant
Quitté par sa mère,
Comme un pauvre enfant
Que rien ne défend,

Vous me laissez là,
Dans ma vie amère;
Vous me laissez là,
Et Dieu voit cela!

Savez-vous qu'un jour
L'homme est seul au monde?
Savez-vous qu'un jour
Il revoit l'amour?

Vous appellerez,
Sans qu'on vous réponde;
Vous appellerez,
Et vous songerez!...

What Did You Do With It?

You had my heart,
made yours my gift.
You had my heart;
luck was our part.

Yours is returned,
I have none left,
Yours is returned,
mine can't be found.

The leaf and the flower
and even the gourd,
the leaf and the flower,
the scent and the color:

What did you do with it,
master and lord?
what did you do with it?
With this sweet benefit?

Like a poor babe
left by her mother,
like a poor babe
no-one can save,

you abandoned me
in bitter weather;
you abandoned me;
this is what God can see.

One day, don't you know
Man walks the world alone?
One day, don't you know
you'll miss our love so.

You'll come a-calling,
but hear from no-one
You'll come a-calling
and you will dream!

Vous viendrez rêvant
Sonner à ma porte;
Ami comme avant,
Vous viendrez rêvant.

Et l'on vous dira :
" Personne !... elle est morte. "
On vous le dira;
Mais qui vous plaindra?

Dreaming you'll drift
to rattle my gate.
As if there were no rift,
dreaming you'll drift.

And they will say to you:
Oh, you seek the late...?
This they will say to you,
but who will pray for you?

Le premier amour

Vous souvient-il de cette jeune amie,
Au regard tendre, au maintien sage et doux?
À peine, hélas ! Au printemps de sa vie,
Son cœur sentit qu'il était fait pour vous.

Point de serment, point de vaine promesse:
Si jeune encore, on ne les connaît pas;
Son âme pure aimait avec ivresse
Et se livrait sans honte et sans combats.

Elle a perdu son idole chérie:
Bonheur si doux a duré moins qu'un jour!
Elle n'est plus au printemps de sa vie,
Elle est encore à son premier amour.

The First Love

Do you recall this girl you once held dear,
her tender look, her manner sweet and true?
Barely, alas. But while her spring was here,
her heart supposed that it was made for you.

Then came the vow, a promise steeped in fiction—
those still young accept such at their name—
and her pure soul adored without restriction.
She gave herself, no struggle and no shame.

She worshipped you, so quick to disappear.
Such sweet good luck endured less than a day!
The springtime of her life's no longer here:
yet even now, her first love still holds sway.

Le berceau d'Hélène.

Qu'a-t-on fait du bocage où rêva mon enfance?
Oh! je le vois toujours! j'y voudrais être encor!
Au milieu des parfums j'y dormais sans défense,
Et le soleil sur lui versait des rayons d'or.
Peut-être qu'à cette heure il colore les roses,
Et que son doux reflet tremble dans le ruisseau.
Viens couler à mes pieds, clair ruisseau qui l'arroses;
Sous tes flots transparents, montre-moi le berceau;
Viens, j'attends ta fraîcheur, j'appelle ton murmure;
      J'écoute, réponds-moi!
Sur tes bords, où les fleurs se fanent sans culture,
Les fleurs ont besoin d'eau, mon cœur sèche sans toi.
Viens, viens me rappeler, dans ta course limpide,
Mes jeux, mes premiers jeux, si chers, si décevants,
Des compagnes d'Hélène un souvenir rapide,
Et leurs rires lointains, faibles jouets des vents.
Si tu veux caresser mon oreille attentive,
N'as-tu pas quelquefois, en poursuivant ton cours,
Lorsqu'elles vont s'asseoir et causer sur ta rive,
N'as-tu pas entendu mon nom dans leurs discours?

Sur les roses peut-être une abeille s'élance:
Je voudrais être abeille et mourir dans les fleurs,
Ou le petit oiseau dont le nid s'y balance:
Il chante, elle est heureuse, et j'ai connu les pleurs.
Je ne pleurais jamais sous sa voûte embaumée;
Une jeune Espérance y dansait sur mes pas:
Elle venait du ciel, dont l'enfance est aimée;
Je dansais avec elle; oh! je ne pleurais pas!
Elle m'avait donné son prisme, don fragile!
J'ai regardé la vie à travers ses couleurs.
Que la vie était belle! et, dans son vol agile,
Que ma jeune Espérance y répandait de fleurs!
Qu'il était beau l'ombrage où j'entendais les muses
Me révéler tout bas leurs promesses confuses;
Où j'osais leur répondre, et de ma faible voix,
Bégayer le serment de suivre un jour leurs lois!

Helene's Birthplace

What has come of the groves where my childhood once dreamed?
Oh I see them forever, still wish I were there!
Without guard I would sleep with their scents everywhere
and upon every hillside the golden sun streamed.
Perhaps at this hour it is tinting each rose
and its soft image ripples the brook into foam.
Oh sweet water that cleanses, come pool at my toes,
for your clear waves roll over the place I call home.
I'm expecting your freshness, invoking your sigh.
       I listen, so talk back!
On the banks, where the blooms without nurture will die,
the flowers need water, my heart's parched from lack.
Oh come and remind me, from your clear bends
of my games, my first games, that were dear though a tease,
bring back to me quickly Helene's childhood friends
and their long ago laughs, now weak toys of the breeze.
If you wish to be kind to my well-focused ear,
now and then, maybe you, as you've gone on your way,
when the chattering girls would sit down with you near,
have heard mentioned my name in the things they would say?

And maybe a honeybee darts at the roses:
like a bee amid flowers I wish I could die
or the sweet little bird who that bird's nest discloses:
he sings, the bee's glad, but I've learned how to cry.
I never did cry in your long-ago glade
when youthful Hope danced with her footsteps in mine:
she came from the sky, which to children is kind,
and I couldn't start crying while she and I swayed.
She had lent me her prism, which I feared to break.
I looked at the world through its spectrum of light.
How beautiful life was! and in its swift flight
my young Hope left bouquets of flowers in her wake.
How lovely the shade where I heard the nine Muses
deliver in whispers their vows and excuses;
where I dared to reply, and in my feeble voice
swore a stuttering oath that their way was my choice.

D'un souvenir si doux l'erreur évanouie
Laisse au fond de mon âme un long étonnement.
C'est une belle aurore à peine épanouie
Qui meurt dans un nuage; et je dis tristement:
Qu'a-t-on fait du bocage où rêva mon enfance?
Oh! j'en parle toujours! j'y voudrais être encor!
Au milieu des parfums j'y dormais sans défense,
Et le soleil sur lui versait des rayons d'or.

Mais au fond du tableau, cherchant des yeux sa proie,
J'ai vu... je vois encor s'avancer le Malheur.
Il errait comme une ombre, il attristait ma joie
      Sous les traits d'un vieux oiseleur;
Et le vieux oiseleur, patiemment avide,
Aux pièges, avant l'aube, attendait les oiseaux;
Et le soir il comptait, avec un ris perfide,
Ses petits prisonniers tremblants sous les réseaux.
      Est-il toujours bien cruel, bien barbare,
Bien sourd à la prière? et, dans sa main avare,
      Plutôt que de l'ouvrir,
Presse-t-il sa victime à la faire mourir?
Ah! Du moins, comme alors, puisse une jeune fille
Courir, en frappant l'air d'une tendre clameur,
Renvoyer dans les cieux la chantante famille,
Et tromper le méchant qui faisait le dormeur!
Dieu! quand on le trompait, quelle était sa colère!
Il fallait fuir : des pleurs ne lui suffisaient pas;
Ou, d'une pitié feinte exigeant le salaire,
Il pardonnait tout haut, il maudissait tout bas.
Au pied d'un vieux rempart, une antique chaumière
      Lui servait de réduit;
Il allait s'y cacher tout seul et sans lumière,
      Comme l'oiseau de nuit.
Un soir, en traversant l'église abandonnée,
Sa voix nomma la Mort. Que sa voix me fit peur!
Je m'envolai tremblante au seuil où j'étais née,
Et j'entendis l'écho rire avec le trompeur.
«Dis, qu'est-ce que la Mort?» demandai-je à ma mère.
«— C'est un vieux oiseleur qui menace toujours.
Tout tombe dans ses rets, ma fille, et les beaux jours
S'éteignent sous ses doigts comme un souffle éphémère.»

The error that's missing from this recollection's
an eternal bewilderment deep in my brain.
Such a beautiful dawn scarcely came to perfection
when it died in a cloud; and I say through my pain:
What has come of the groves where my childhood once dreamed?
Oh I speak of them always, still wish I were there!
Without guard I would sleep with their scents everywhere
and upon every hillside the golden sun streamed.

Yet behind the montage, with his eyes on his snare,
I saw...I still see that Bad Luck's drawing up.
He shifted like shadows and poisoned my cup
with a grizzled old bird-catcher's air.
And the grizzled old bird-catcher, patiently greedy,
awaited the birds at his traps, before dawn,
and at night tallied up, while his cackle grew reedy
his captives behind their bars, small and forlorn.
          Is he always so vulgar and sly,
so deaf to our prayers that in his thick fist
          rather than let it fly
he squeezes his prey till it cannot exist.
Oh if only, as once was, a young girl could run,
disturbing the heavens with judicious cries
and driving the singing crowd into the sun,
deceiving the evil one, caught by surprise.
Oh God! When she fooled him how madly he burned.
The girl had to run, for her tears gained no ground,
Or pretending some pity to yield a return,
he forgave her out loud as he cursed with no sound.
At the foot of a once gracious castle a shed
          made a roof for his head;
he went there to hide all alone without light
          like a bird of the night.
One dusk as I passed the old church—now a shambles
his voice called out Death. How his voice made me tremble!
I ran away, cold, to the place I was weaned
but I heard how the echo laughed on with the fiend.
So I asked of my mother: Please, what is this Death?—
It's a grizzled old bird-catcher—full of malaise.
All fall in his traps, my dear, and the good days
are put out by his thumbs like ephemeral breath.

Je demeurai pensive et triste sur son sein.
Depuis, j'allai m'asseoir aux tombes délaissées:
Leur tranquille silence éveillait mes pensées;
Y cueillir une fleur me semblait un larcin.
L'aquilon m'effrayait de ses soupirs funèbres.
La voix, toujours la voix, m'annonçait le Malheur;
Et quand je l'entendais passer dans les ténèbres,
Je disais: «C'est la Mort, ou le vieux oiseleur.»

Mais tout change: l'autan fait place aux vents propices,
      La nuit fait place au jour;
La verdure, au printemps, couvre les précipices,
Et l'hirondelle heureuse y chante son retour:
Je revis le berceau, le soleil et les roses;
Ruisseau, tu m'appelais, je m'élançai vers toi:
Je t'appelle à mon tour, clair ruisseau qui l'arroses;
      J'écoute, réponds-moi!
Qu'a-t-on fait du bocage où rêva mon enfance?
Oh! je le vois toujours! j'y voudrais être encor!
Au milieu des parfums j'y dormais sans défense,
Et le soleil sur lui versait des rayons d'or!

I remained sad and thoughtful, my head on her breast,
then I went to sit down on a tumbledown vault;
my thoughts were awoken in this place of rest;
simply picking a flower seemed to me like a fault.
The north wind alarmed me with funeral moans.
The voice, still the voice, said *Bad Luck* with each breath;
and I said, as it passed by the shadowy stones:
it's that grizzled old bird-catcher that we call Death.

But everything changes, and warmer winds lift;
  bright day displaces black;
In the spring, the green grass grows all over the cliffs
and the swallow is happy to sing that he's back.
I saw again sunshine, my birthplace and roses.
Oh brook, you were calling, I ran down the track,
I called you in turn, oh sweet water that cleanses.
  I listen, so talk back!
What has come of the groves where my childhood once dreamed?
Oh I see them forever, still wish I were there!
Without guard I would sleep with their scents everywhere
and upon every hillside the golden sun streamed.

La fontaine

Et moi je n'aime plus la fontaine d'eau vive,
Dont la molle fraîcheur m'attirait vers le soir;
Et, comme l'autre été, dormeuse, sur sa rive
     Je ne vais plus m'asseoir.

Dans les saules émus passe-t-elle affaiblie?
Je fuis vers le sentier qui ramène au hameau,
Sans oser regarder si du plus jeune ormeau
Elle baigne l'écorce et le nom que j'oublie!
Que son cristal mouvant épure les zéphyrs,
Que la fleur soit contente en s' y voyant éclore,
Qu'un front riant s'admire en son eau qu'il colore,
L'eau ne roulera plus au bruit de mes soupirs.

Je l'aimais l'autre été, j'aimais tout! Simple et tendre,
Je croyais tout sincère à l'égal de mon cœur:
Eh bien! Comme une voix que j' y venais entendre,
À présent tout me semble infidèle et moqueur.

     Cette murmurante fontaine,
     Appelant un secret qu'elle ne comprend pas,
     Semblait me demander ma peine,
     Et son charme égarait mes pas.

Elle est douce à l'oreille: oh! C'est qu'elle est flatteuse.
Une image nouvelle y glisse tous les jours.
Elle parle... elle est libre... hélas! Elle est heureuse;
Mais libre, elle est ingrate et s'échappe toujours.

Et moi je n'aime plus la fontaine d'eau vive,
Dont la molle fraîcheur m'attirait vers le soir,
Et, comme l'autre été, rêveuse, sur sa rive
     Je ne vais plus m'asseoir.

The Spring

I no longer love the limpid water spring,
whose soft freshness in the evenings pulled me in;
unlike last summer, eyes closing, by her brink
      I won't sit down again.

By the sad willows does she yet trickle at all?
I fly down the path that leads to the tiny town
without daring to see if she washes the bark down
on the youngest elm, and the one I won't recall.
Though her liquid crystal purify the breeze,
and the flower rejoice to see her source appear,
and a cheerful face admire its reflection here,
her water will flow no more to the sound of my sighs.

Last summer, I loved her and everything. Simple and caring—
I truly believed my heart could have no peer:
Ah well, like a voice there, which I soon came to hear,
now everything seems faithless and full of jeering.

      This spring that babbles,
      naming a secret she doesn't fully know,
      seems to ask about my troubles,
      and her charm lures me off my road.

She is easy on the ears: oh, full of compliments!
A new image glides over her every day.
She talks...she is free...alas! she is content;
but free, ungratefully she runs away.

I no longer love the limpid water spring,
whose soft freshness in the evenings pulled me in;
unlike last summer, dreaming, by her brink
      I won't sit down again.

A Délie (IV)

Toi, dont jamais les larmes
N'ont terni la beauté,
Enveloppe tes charmes,
Enchaîne ta gaieté;
Que ta grâce divine,
Sous un voile de deuil,
S'abandonne et s'incline
Sur le bord d'un cercueil!

Quitte cette guirlande
Qui pare tes attraits;
Laisse-la pour offrande
A ce jeune Cyprès:
C'est ici le mélange
Des roses et des pleurs;
C'est l'asile d'un ange
Qu'il dorme sous des fleurs;

Vois-tu, sous l'herbe tendre,
Ce précoce tombeau?
La mon Cœur vient attendre
Qu'on en creuse un nouveau.
Oui, mon fils! L'arbre sombre
Qui se penche vers toi,
En te gardant son ombre,
Croitra bientôt sur moi!

Toi, dont jamais les larmes
N'ont terni la beauté,
Enveloppe tes charmes,
Enchaîne ta gaieté.
Adieu, belle Délie;
Je te rends au plaisir;
Retourne vers la vie,
Et laisse-moi mourir.

To Delia (IV)

You, whose tears I'm sure
have rarely stained your beauty,
veil, for once, your allure,
rein in your gaiety.
How your divine grace
slips as you lean towards,
(parting your devil's lace),
this little coffin's boards.

Set your wreath adrift
and lose its flattery:
leave it as a gift
to this young Cyprus tree.
Here you see the muddles
of roses and of tears,
where an angel huddles
asleep beneath the flowers.

A grave dug far too soon
lies beneath soft dirt;
there, my heart has been
waiting for further hurt.
Yes, my son! The tree
which leans above you sternly
and guards him in its lee
will soon fall into me.

You, whose tears I'm sure
have rarely stained your beauty,
veil, for once, your allure,
rein in your gaiety.
Bye Delia, so pretty,
I release you to your joy;
please go back to the city,
let me die with my boy.

Hippolyte

La mère et l'enfant

Quand j'ai grondé mon fils, je me cache et je pleure.
Qui suis-je, pour punir, moi, roseau devant Dieu,
Pour devancer le temps qui nous gronde à toute heure,
Et crie a tous: Prends garde; il faudra dire adieu!

Mourir avec le poids d'une parole amère,
D'une larme d'enfant que l'on a fait couler,
Que l'on sent sur son cœur incessamment rouler!
Est-ce donc pour ce droit que l'on veut être mère?

Est-ce donc là le prix des immenses douleurs
Dont nous avons payé leur présence adorée?
De ce pas sur la tombe encor toute navrée,
Dieu! laissez-nous donc vivre et respirer nos fleurs!

Laissez-nous contempler à deux genoux la tige,
Qui veut se lever seule et frémît d'obéir,
Qui veut sa liberté, son plaisir, doux vertige.
Tout ce qui nait, mon Dieu! tend ses bras au plaisir.

Laissez-nous seulement, ardentes sentinelles,
Écarter leurs dangers qu'ils aiment, si petits;
Si forts a repousser nos forces maternelles,
De la fierté de l'homme innocents apprentis.

Purifiez un peu ce monde, ou chaque haleine
A l'entour de nos fruits soufflé un air plein de feu;
Préservez le lait pur dont leur âme était pleine;
Alors nous guiderons l'ange par un cheveu.

Beaux anges mutinés qui bravez nos tendresses,
Dont les jours, dont les nuits tièdes de nos caresses,
Loin de vos nids plumeux brulent de s'envoler,
Où dormirez-vous mieux pour vous en consoler?

Hippolyte

The Mother and the Child

When I've rebuked my son, I hide and cry.
A reed beside our God, dare I condemn,
advance the time, when punishment has no end,
which shouts at each: Prepare to say goodbye!

To die beneath the weight of a bitter phrase,
of an infant's tear which one has caused to fall,
which one feels rolling over one's heart for days!
Is it for this one craved a mother's role?

Is this the wealth of unimaginable hurt
which we have paid to have these dear ones near us?
Lord, not this foot in the horrible grave dirt,
let us live and breathe our flowers—hear us!

Let us ponder this stem upon our knees:
it wants to grow alone, shakes to obey,
wants its freedom, its excitement, joy.
Everything born, my God, reaches for bliss.

Let us be cautious, watching over them,
push back the dangers these small ones go courting,
let our maternal force be strong at thwarting
these naïve learners with the pride of men.

Cleanse a little this world, where in each gulp
our sweet offspring inhale fire-ridden air;
Preserve the pure milk that fills their souls up;
Thus we'll guide each angel by one hair.

Beautiful mutinous angels who let us touch you
through days and nights, lukewarm as we clutch you,
burning to fly off far from your feathery nest,
where will you find better comfort in your rest?

La mère, n'est-ce pas un long baiser de l'âme,
Un baiser qui jamais ne dit non, ni demain?
Faut-il ses jours? Seigneur! Les voila dans sa main:
Prenez-les pour l'enfant de cette heureuse femme.

Enfant! mot qui peut dire: Amour! ciel! ou martyr!
Couronne des berceaux! auréole d'épouse!
Saint orgueil! nœud du sang, éternité jalouse,
Dieu vous fait trop de pleurs pour vous anéantir.

C'est notre âme en dehors, en robe d'innocence,
Hélas! Comme la vit ma mère a ma naissance:
Et si je la contemple avec d'humides yeux,
C'est que la terre est triste, et que l'âme est des cieux!

O femmes! aimez-vous par vos secrets de larmes,
Par vos devoirs sans bruit ou s'effeuillent vos charmes;
Apres vos jours d'encens dont j'ai bu la douceur,
Quand vous aurez souffert, appelez-moi: Ma sœur!

A mother, isn't one a long kiss to your soul,
a kiss that utters neither Tomorrow nor No?
Her days not hers? Master! She gives them smiling:
take them for this happy woman's darling.

Child! The word can mean: Love! sky! or martyr!
Wreath of cradles! Halo of matrimony!
Sainted pride! Blood-knot, jealous eternity,
God makes you too full of tears to hurt you.

It's our own soul outside us, in innocent guise,
alas! My mother saw it thus at my birth
and if I consider this with moistened eyes
it's because such souls are heavenly on this sad earth.

O women, love on through hidden misery,
through the silent efforts which fade your bloom.
Beyond the sweetness we've shared in the womb,
when you've suffered, call me Sister, as we'll be.

La couronne effeuillée

J'irai, j'irai porter ma couronne effeuillée
Au jardin de mon père où revit toute fleur;
J'y répandrai longtemps mon âme agenouillée:
Mon père a des secrets pour vaincre la douleur.

J'irai, j'irai lui dire au moins avec mes larmes:
«Regardez, j'ai souffert...» Il me regardera,
Et sous mes jours changés, sous mes pâleurs sans charmes,
Parce qu'il est mon père, il me reconnaîtra.

Il dira: «C'est donc vous, chère âme désolée;
La terre manque-t-elle à vos pas égarés?
Chère âme, je suis Dieu: ne soyez plus troublée;
Voici votre maison, voici mon cœur, entrez!»

Ô clémence! Ô douceur! Ô saint refuge! Ô Père!
Votre enfant qui pleurait, vous l'avez entendu!
Je vous obtiens déjà, puisque je vous espère
Et que vous possédez tout ce que j'ai perdu.

Vous ne rejetez pas la fleur qui n'est plus belle;
Ce crime de la terre au ciel est pardonné.
Vous ne maudirez pas votre enfant infidèle,
Non d'avoir rien vendu, mais d'avoir tout donné.

The Withered Wreath

I'll go, I'll go, and bring my withered wreath
to my father's garden, which revives all flowers.
There, on my knees, I'll purge my soul for hours.
My father has secrets that triumph over grief.

I'll go, I'll go, and say, at least with tears,
"See, I have suffered..." He will stare at me,
and despite my faded looks, changed by the years,
because he is my father, he'll know it's me.

He'll say, "At last! Dear saddened soul, you're here!
Beneath your straying steps, does earth give way?
Don't be so desolate. I'm God, my dear—
Here is my heart, your home, come in and stay."

O mercy! O sweetness! holy refuge! father!
You have heard your weeping child's lament.
Because of my hope, you're mine to rediscover,
also, because you have all I've misspent.

You don't reject this flower in its decay—
such earthly crime's no sin in paradise.
Your child of little faith won't be chastised,
not for selling nothing, but for giving all away.

Renoncement

Pardonnez-moi, Seigneur, mon visage attristé,
Vous qui l'aviez formé de sourire et de charmes;
Mais sous le front joyeux vous aviez mis les larmes,
Et de vos dons, Seigneur, ce don seul m'est resté.

C'est le moins envié, c'est le meilleur peut-être:
Je n'ai plus à mourir à mes liens de fleurs;
Ils vous sont tous rendus, cher auteur de mon être,
Et je n'ai plus à moi que le sel de mes pleurs.

Les fleurs sont pour l'enfant; le sel est pour la femme;
Faites-en l'innocence et trempez-y mes jours.
Seigneur! quand tout ce sel aura lavé mon âme,
Vous me rendrez un cœur pour vous aimer toujours!

Tous mes étonnements sont finis sur la terre,
Tous mes adieux sont faits, l'âme est prête à jaillir,
Pour atteindre à ses fruits protégés de mystère
Que la pudique mort a seule osé cueillir,

O Sauveur! soyez tendre au moins à d'autres mères,
Par amour pour la vôtre et par pitié pour nous!
Baptisez leurs enfants de nos larmes amères,
Et relevez les miens tombés à vos genoux!

Que mon nom ne soit rien qu'une ombre douce et vaine,
Qu'il ne cause jamais ni l'effroi ni la peine!
Qu'un indigent l'emporte après m'avoir parlé
Et le garde longtemps dans son cœur consolé!

Renunciation

Forgive me, Lord, for my face full of sadness,
you who made it full of charm and gladness;
but under this joyful brow you have set tears,
and of your gifts, Lord, only this perseveres.

It's the least envied, maybe it's the better:
I do not have to die in my chains of flowers;
they've given all back to you, my dear begetter
and I have nothing left but the salt of my tears.

Flowers for the child, salt for the woman.
Steep my days in the innocence thus made.
Lord, when all this salt has cleansed this human,
you'll give me back a heart to love you always.

All my astonishments on earth are over.
All my goodbyes are done. My soul is fit to burst,
to reach the fruits mystery keeps covered
that only discreet death has dared to harvest.

O Savior, be gentle to other mothers at least,
out of love for your own and pity for us.
Baptize their children with our bitter tears
and lift my fallen ones onto your knees.

May my name be nothing but a soft and hollow token.
May it never cause either trouble or alarm.
May a beggar take it after we have spoken,
and keep it a long time in his heart, now calm.

Les sanglots

Ah! l'enfer est ici! l'autre me fait moins peur.
Pourtant le purgatoire inquiète mon cœur.

On m'en a trop parlé pour que ce nom funeste
Sur un si faible cœur ne serpente et ne reste.

Et quand le flot des jours me défait fleur à fleur.
Je vois le purgatoire au fond de ma pâleur.

S'ils ont dit vrai, c'est là qu'il faut aller s'éteindre,
O Dieu de toute vie! avant de vous atteindre.

C'est là qu'il faut descendre, et sans lune et sans jour.
Sous le poids de la crainte et la croix de l'amour;

Pour entendre gémir les âmes condamnées
Sans pouvoir dire: allez! vous êtes pardonnées;

Sans pouvoir les tarir, ô douleur des douleurs!
Sentir filtrer partout les sanglots et les pleurs;

Se heurter dans la nuit des cages cellulaires
Que nulle aube ne teint de ses prunelles claires;

Ne savoir où crier au Sauveur méconnu:
«Hélas! mon doux Sauveur, n'êtes-vous pas venu?»

Ah! j'ai peur d'avoir peur, d'avoir froid, je me cache
Comme un oiseau tombé qui tremble qu'on l'attache.

Je rouvre tristement mes bras au souvenir...
Mais c'est le purgatoire et je le sens venir.

C'est là que je me rêve après la mort menée
Comme une esclave en faute au bout de sa journée,

Cachant sous ses deux mains son front pâle et flétri
Et marchant sur son cœur par la terre meurtri.

The Sobbing

Ah! Hell's here! I fear the other less.
And yet it's purgatory that gives me stress.

I've heard too much of it for the lethal term
not to rest in my weak heart like a worm.

When the flood of days undoes me flower by flower,
I make out purgatory beneath my pallor.

It's there one goes to fade, if what's said is true,
O God of all that lives, before reaching you.

Without the moon or day, to there one's led
under the cross of love and the weight of dread;

in order to hear the moans of those condemned,
unable to say the words, "Go on! You're pardoned";

sensing all around, O deepest grief,
the sobbing and tears, unable to give relief;

colliding in the prison cells' dark night,
which no sunrise can pierce however bright;

not seeing where to call to an ill-known one,
"Alas! My Savior sweet, have you not come?"

I'm scared to be afraid, to be cold. I hide
like a fallen bird which trembles at your side.

Sadly I spread my arms at the memory
but it is purgatory and I feel it with me.

I dream I'm there, after the stolen death,
just like a rule-breaking slave at day's last breath,

hiding his pale, tense brow in both his hands,
and walking on his heart bruised by these lands.

C'est là que je m'en vais au-devant de moi-même
N'osant y souhaiter rien de tout ce que j'aime.

Je n'aurais donc plus rien de charmant dans le cœur
Que le lointain écho de leur vivant bonheur.

Ciel! où m'en irai-je
Sans pieds pour courir?
Ciel! où frapperai-je
Sans clé pour ouvrir?

Sous l'arrêt éternel repoussant ma prière
Jamais plus le soleil n'atteindra ma paupière

Pour ressuyer du monde et des tableaux affreux
Qui font baisser partout mes regards douloureux.

Plus de soleil! Pourquoi? Cette lumière aimée
Aux méchants de la terre est pourtant allumée;

Sur un pauvre coupable à l'échafaud conduit
Comme un doux «viens à moi» l'orbe s'épanche et luit.

Plus de feu nulle part! Plus d'oiseaux dans l'espace!
Plus d'Ave Maria dans la brise qui passe!

Au bord des lacs taris plus un roseau mouvant!
Plus d'air pour soutenir un atome vivant!

Ces fruits que tout ingrat sent fondre sous sa lèvre
Ne feront plus couler leurs fraîcheurs dans ma fièvre;

Et de mon cœur absent qui viendra m'oppresser
J'amasserai les pleurs sans pouvoir les verser.

Ciel! où m'en irai-je
Sans pieds pour courir?
Ciel! où frapperai-je
Sans clé pour ouvrir?

Plus de ces souvenirs qui m'emplissent de larmes,
Si vivants que toujours je vivrais de leurs charmes;

It's there that I go to meet with my own self
not daring to wish there for anyone I love.

So I'd have nothing sweeter in my heart
than their living fortune echoing from afar.

Heaven! Where do I go
with no feet to bear my weight?
Heaven! Where do I knock
with no key to open your gate?

Repeating my prayer beneath eternal law
that the sun may not reach my pupils any more

to wipe from the world and these atrocious views
all that my unhappy gaze tries to refuse.

No more sun! Why? This beloved light
even makes Earth's sinners' daytimes bright;

like a soft summons the orb pours light around
the unlucky criminal who's scaffold-bound.

No more fire at all! No more birds in the sky!
No more Ave Marias on the breeze passing by!

Beside the dried up lakes no waving reeds!
No air to give what any live cell needs!

These melting fruits my mouth claims as its due
won't have their freshness to work my fever through,

and from my heart both absent and oppressing
I'll gather tears I have no way of shedding.

Heaven! Where do I go
with no feet to bear my weight?
Heaven! Where do I knock
with no key to open your gate?

No more memories causing tears to fall,
so real that they still have me in their thrall.

Plus de famille, au soir, assise sur le seuil
Pour bénir son sommeil chantant devant l'aïeul;

Plus de timbre adoré dont la grâce invincible
Eût forcé le néant à devenir sensible;

Plus de livres divins comme effeuillés des cieux
Concerts que tous mes sens écoutaient par mes yeux

Ainsi n'oser mourir quand on n'ose plus vivre
Ni chercher dans la mort un ami qui délivre!

O parents, pourquoi donc vos fleurs sur nos berceaux
Si le ciel a maudit l'arbre et les arbrisseaux?

Ciel! où m'en irai-je
Sans pieds pour courir?
Ciel! où frapperai-je
Sans clé pour ouvrir?

Sous la croix qui s'incline à l'âme prosternée
Punie après la mort du malheur d'être née!

Mais quoi! dans cette mort qui se sent expirer
Si quelque cri lointain me disait d'espérer,

Si dans ce ciel éteint quelque étoile pâlie
Envoyait sa lueur à ma mélancolie?

Sous ces arceaux tendus d'ombre et de désespoir
Si des yeux inquiets s'allumaient pour me voir?

Oh! ce serait ma mère intrépide et bénie
Descendant réclamer sa fille assez punie.

Oui! ce serait ma mère ayant attendri Dieu
Qui viendra me sauver de cet horrible lieu,

Et relever au vent de la jeune espérance
Son dernier fruit tombé mordu par la souffrance.

Je sentirai ses bras si beaux, si doux, si forts,
M'étreindre et m'enlever dans ses puissants efforts;

No more family singing by the door
before grandpa to help him sleep some more.

No more beloved voice whose supreme grace
forced the universe from empty space.

No more divine books like art from the skies,
concerts that all my senses hear with my eyes.

Thus when life overwhelms, not to risk the end,
nor to seek in death a delivering friend.

O parents! Why put those flowers on our cribs
if heaven has cursed the tree and all its shrubs?

Heaven! Where do I go
with no feet to bear my weight?
Heaven! Where do I knock
with no key to open your gate?

Beneath the cross which tilts at the prostrate form
of a dead man blamed for his bad luck to be born.

But what if, in this death so aware of dying,
I hear some words of hope in distant crying:

if in this blacked-out sky some feeble sun
sends its rays towards me as I mourn?

Under these arches of shade and hopelessness
if anxious eyes lit up to scan my face?

Oh! That would be my mother, brave and blessed,
coming to lay my punishment to rest.

Yes, that will be my mother who's moved God
so she can save me from this place of dread

and on youth's hopeful canopy set right
its final windfall hurt by suffering's bite.

I'll feel her soft arms, strong and full of grace,
lift me in her powerful embrace.

Je sentirai couler dans mes naissantes ailes
L'air pur qui fait monter les libres hirondelles.

Et ma mère en fuyant pour ne plus revenir
M'emportera vivante à travers l'avenir!

Mais avant de quitter les mortelles campagnes
Nous irons appeler des âmes pour compagnes,

Au bout du champ funèbre où j'ai mis tant de fleurs.
Nous ébattre aux parfums qui sont nés de mes pleurs.

Et nous aurons des voix, des transports et des flammes
Pour crier: Venez-vous? à ces dolentes âmes.

«Venez-vous vers l'été qui fait tout refleurir.
Où nous allons aimer sans pleurer, sans mourir?

«Venez, venez voir Dieu! nous sommes ses colombes.
Jetez-là vos linceuls, les cieux n'ont plus de tombes,

«Le Sépulcre est rompu par l'éternel amour,
Ma mère nous enfante à l'éternel séjour!»

And through my new wings I'll feel the pure air
coursing, which makes the boundless swallows soar.

And, fleeing never to return, my mother
will carry me living across into the future!

But before we leave our mortal struggles for dust,
we'll call some souls to come along with us.

At the foot of the burial field I've strewn with flowers,
we'll frolic in the scents born from my tears,

and we shall have the fire, the means, and the voice,
to cry to these sad ones, "Are you coming with us?"

"Are you coming to the summer full of flowers,
where we'll be free to love without death or tears?"

"Come! Come see the Lord. We are his doves.
Throw off your shrouds, for Heaven has no graves."

"The Tomb is broken by this endless love.
My mother's endless care awaits above."

L'adieu tout bas

"Quoi! chanter quand l'amour, quand la douleur déchire!
Chanter, le mort dans l'âme et les pleurs dans les yeux!" ~Jean Polonius

Autant que moi-même,
En quittant ces lieux,
Cherchez qui vous aime
Et vous plaise mieux!

Eloignez la flamme
Qui nourrit mes pleurs,
Car je n'ai qu'une âme
Pour tant de douleurs!

La raison regarde
A trop d'amitié;
J'en pris, par mégarde,
Plus de la moitié!

Dormez à ma plainte,
Quand j'écris tout bas
Ces mots que ma crainte
N'exhalera pas!

La femme qui pleure
Trahit son pouvoir;
Il faut qu'elle meure
Sans le laisser voir!

Quand le cœur sommeille
Frappé de langueur,
Ce n'est pas l'oreille
Qui comprend le cœur!

Il est un langage
Appris par les yeux;
Nos yeux, page a page,
Y lurent les cieux!

The Whispered Goodbye

"What! Sing when love, when grief rips through!
Sing, death in the soul and tears in the eyes!" ~Jean Polonius

Much as I plan to,
leaving this coast,
look for one to love
and please you the most.

Take away the flame
that feeds my crying,
since I've just one soul
for all this sighing.

We think too much about
those for whom we care.
By accident I've done
more than my share.

Sleep through my complaint
when secretly I write
these words that my fear
won't let me recite.

Women who cry
betray their power.
It's better to die
than let weakness flower.

When the heart dozes,
riven by malaise,
it's not the ear that knows
the heart's special ways.

It is a language
learned by the eyes.
Our eyes, page by page,
draw heavenly skies

C'est un livre d'ange,
Quand on est aimé:
Si l'un des deux change,
Le livre est fermé!

It's a book of angels
to have a true lover.
When that lover changes
the book is over.

Ma chambre

Ma demeure est haute,
Donnant sur les cieux;
La lune en est l'hôte,
Pâle et sérieux:
En bas que l'on sonne,
Qu'importe aujourd'hui
Ce n'est plus personne,
Quand ce n'est plus lui!

Aux autres cachée,
Je brode mes fleurs;
Sans être fâchée,
Mon âme est en pleurs;
Le ciel bleu sans voiles,
Je le vois d'ici ;
Je vois les étoiles
Mais l'orage aussi!

Vis-à-vis la mienne
Une chaise attend:
Elle fut la sienne,
La nôtre un instant;
D'un ruban signée,
Cette chaise est là,
Toute résignée,
Comme me voilà!

My Room

It's on the top floor,
and looks out on the sky;
the moon holds the door,
pallid and shy.
The doorbell below
means nothing today.
There's none I would know
since he's gone away.

Hidden from the rest
I work with my thread
I may not seem stressed
but what tears I've shed!
I can see from up here
an expanse of clear blue,
I see stars reappear
and the storms coming too.

I sit here alone
in one of two chairs;
the other, his own,
for a short while—ours.
Ribbon-entwined,
this chair must wait,
fully resigned
like me to my fate.

Élégie

Il fait nuit: le vent souffle et passe dans ma lyre;
Ma lyre tristement s'éveille auprès de moi:
On dirait qu'elle pleure un tourment, un délire,
On dirait qu'elle essaie à se plaindre de toi,
De toi, qu'elle appelait pour m'aider à t'attendre,
Qui la rendis si vraie, et par malheur si tendre!
Car tu ne peux ravir à ses accords touchants
Ton nom, toujours ton nom, qui courait dans mes chants.
Elle ne le dit plus ce nom doux et sonore,
Elle ne le dit plus, elle le pleure encore!
Combien elle a frémi, combien elle a chanté,
Sous les prompts battements de mon cœur agité,
Alors que, dans l'orgueil des amantes aimées,
Je confiais mon âme aux cordes animées!
Je croyais que les cieux ne donnaient tant d'amour,
Que pour en pénétrer une autre âme à son tour!

Ah! J'aurais dû mourir, doucement endormie,
Dans cette erreur charmante où j'étais ton amie.
Devrait-on s'éveiller de ces rêves confus,
Pour y penser toujours, et pour n'y croire plus!

Elegy

It's night: the soft wind blows and strums my lyre;
my wretched lyre of her own accord comes to:
One would say she cries in fever and despair;
one would say she tries to remonstrate with you.

With you, whom she'd name to help my waiting pass,
who made her so true, and so in love, alas!
For you cannot hear, in her pitiful refrain
the name shot through my songs again and again.
She says it no more, this ringing name, once dear;
she says it no more, she sobs it through her tears!
How often has she quivered, how often hummed
under my trembling heartbeat's rapid drum,
while I, with pride in love felt and received
poured out my soul on strings that seemed to breathe.
I thought that heaven-sent loving this intense
must pierce in turn its recipient's defense.

I should have died, asleep in this sweet world
of charming error where I was your girl.
Must one awake from dreams so ill-conceived,
to think of them always, and yet disbelieve?

About the Author

Anna M. Evans' poems have appeared in the *Harvard Review, Atlanta Review, Rattle, American Arts Quarterly,* and *32 Poems.* She gained her MFA from Bennington College, and is the Editor of *The Raintown Review.* Recipient of Fellowships from the MacDowell Artists' Colony and the Virginia Center for the Creative Arts, and winner of the 2012 Rattle Poetry Prize Readers' Choice Award, she currently teaches at West Windsor Art Center and Richard Stockton College of New Jersey. Her new sonnet collection, *Sisters & Courtesans,* is forthcoming from White Violet Press. Visit her online at www.annamevans.com.

Made in the USA
San Bernardino, CA
04 April 2020